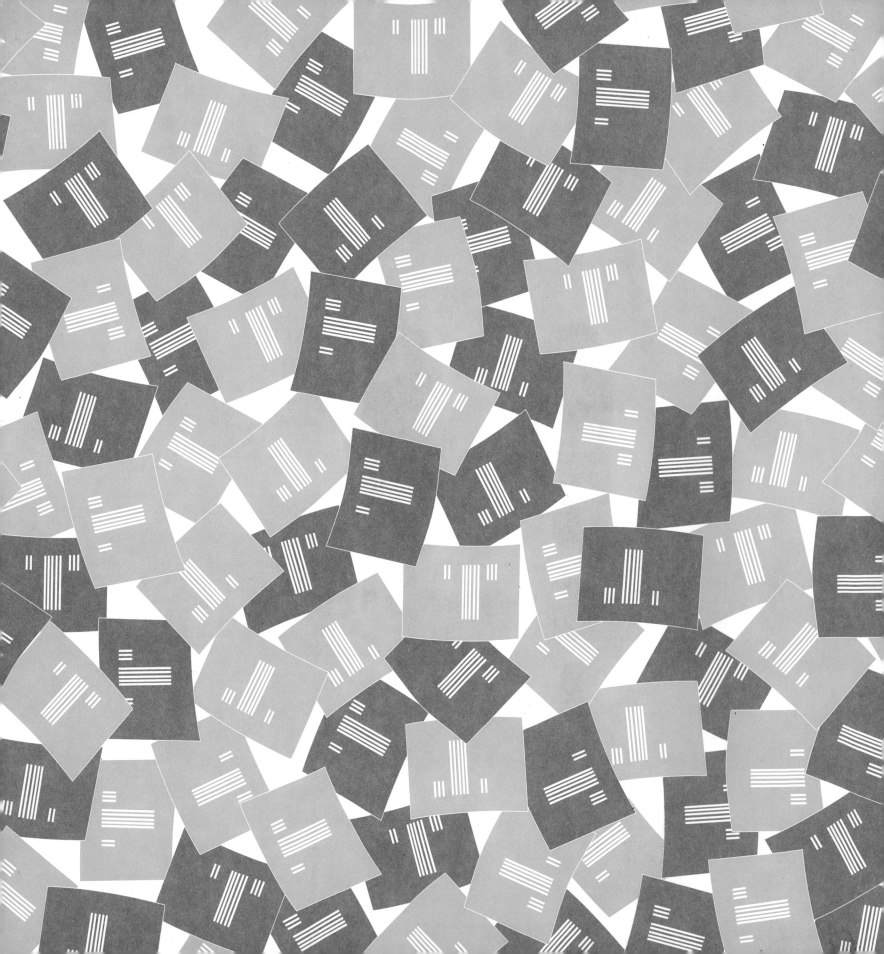

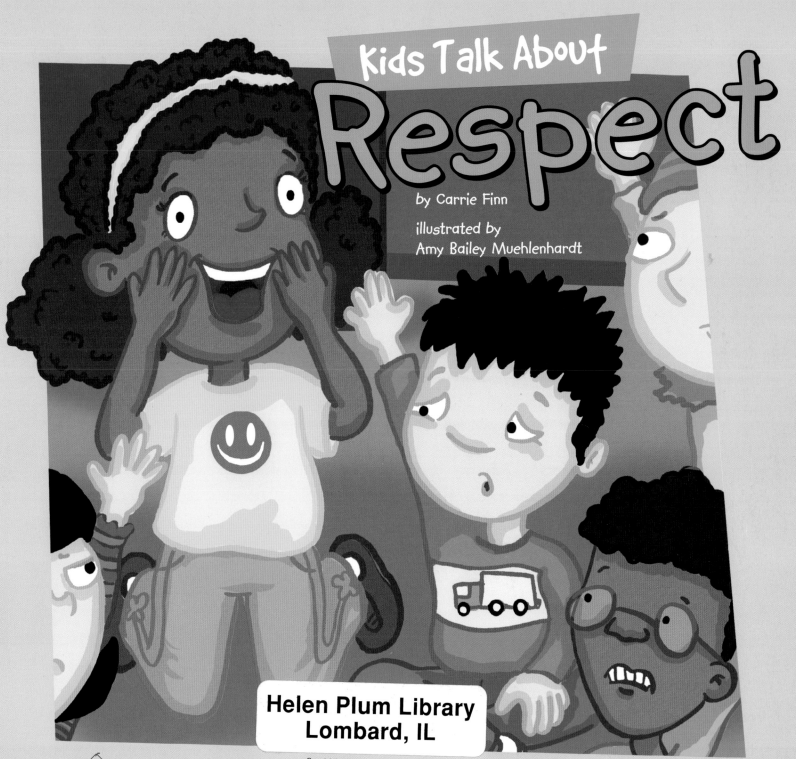

Kids Talk About
Respect

by Carrie Finn

illustrated by
Amy Bailey Muehlenhardt

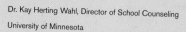

PICTURE WINDOW BOOKS
Minneapolis, Minnesota

Special thanks to our advisers for their expertise:

Dr. Kay Herting Wahl, Director of School Counseling
University of Minnesota

Susan Kesselring, M.A., Literacy Educator
Rosemount–Apple Valley–Eagan (Minnesota) School District

Editor: Christianne Jones

Designer: Joe Anderson

Page Production: Brandie Shoemaker

Editorial Director: Carol Jones

Creative Director: Keith Griffin

The illustrations in this book were created digitally.

Picture Window Books

5115 Excelsior Boulevard

Suite 232

Minneapolis, MN 55416

877-845-8392

www.picturewindowbooks.com

Photo Credit: Alex Wong/Getty Images, page 30

Library of Congress Cataloging-in-Publication Data

Finn, Carrie.

Kids talk about respect / by Carrie Finn ; illustrated by Amy Bailey Muehlenhardt.

p. cm. — (Kids talk junior)

Includes bibliographical references and index.

ISBN-13: 978-1-4048-2318-1 (hardcover)

ISBN-10: 1-4048-2318-2 (hardcover)

1. Respect—Juvenile literature. I. Muehlenhardt, Amy Bailey, 1974- ill. II. Title. III. Series.

BJ1533.R4F56 2007

179'.9—dc22
2006003402

Kids Talk Jr.

COUNSELOR: Kendra

Hi, Friends!

My name is Kendra Kemp. I'm in the fifth grade at Newton Elementary School. My friends call me "Kind Kendra." My favorite thing to do is to give advice and help others.

Respect is when you treat someone or something in a good way. There are many ways to show respect in our daily lives. Read my advice on being respectful.

Sincerely,

Kendra

Dear Kendra,

When we go on picnics, we always bring our garbage home with us. Why don't we just leave it at the park?

Daria

Kids Talk Jr.

COUNSELOR: Kendra

Dear Daria,

You are showing respect for the environment. Our planet should be treated well. It's important to pick up trash and to recycle.

Kendra

Dear Kendra,

Why do I always have to say "please" and "thank you"?

Beth

Kids Talk Jr.

COUNSELOR: Kendra

Dear Beth,

When you say "please" or "thank you," you are showing respect and good manners. Good manners show that you really appreciate what someone has done for you.

Kendra

Dear Kendra,

My sister yelled at me for practicing piano while she was watching TV. What did I do wrong?

Garth

COUNSELOR: Kendra

Dear Garth,

As long as you asked permission, you didn't do anything wrong. Your sister needs to show respect for your time at the piano. She can turn off the TV and play outside while you practice piano.

Kendra

Dear Kendra,

My brother thinks it's funny to pull our dog's tail. How can I make him stop?

Marc

Kids Talk Jr.

COUNSELOR: Kendra

Dear Marc,

You need to tell your brother that animals deserve respect, too. Ask your brother how he feels when someone pulls his hair. I'll bet he doesn't like it at all!

Kendra

Dear Kendra,

Sometimes I cut through my neighbor's yard on my way home from school. Do you think he cares?

Leif

alk Jr.

COUNSELOR: Kendra

Dear Leif,

It is important to respect other people's property. If you aren't sure if your neighbor is OK with you cutting across his yard, you need to ask him.

Kendra

Dear Kendra,

Why do I have to raise my hand in class when I know the answer? Why can't I just say it?

Sheryl

Kids Talk Jr.

COUNSELOR: Kendra

Dear Sheryl,

If you shout out the answer, you're not respecting your teacher's rules. You aren't respecting your classmates, either. When you raise your hand, you are showing respect for everyone and for the rules.

Kendra

Dear Kendra,

I want to give my friend a present for Christmas, but she doesn't celebrate Christmas. What can I do?

Olivia

Kids Talk Jr.

COUNSELOR: Kendra

Dear Olivia,

Ask your friend if she celebrates a different holiday. It is important to respect the traditions her family has. You may want to learn more about the holiday that she celebrates.

Kendra

Dear Kendra,

I really hate brushing my teeth. Why do I have to do it?

Pedro

Kids Talk Jr.

COUNSELOR: Kendra

Dear Pedro,

When you brush your teeth, you are showing respect for your body. It's important to take care of yourself. You should brush your teeth and hair, exercise, eat healthy food, and wear a helmet when you ride your bike.

Kendra

Dear Kendra,

My dad wants me to visit my great grandpa every week. Why should I do that?

Lizzie

Kids Talk Jr.

COUNSELOR: Kendra

Dear Lizzie,

It's polite to respect your elders. Think of all the amazing things you could learn from your great grandpa. I'll bet that he has done and seen some amazing things in his lifetime!

Kendra

Dear Kendra,

Why do people stand when they recite the Pledge of Allegiance or sing the "Star-Spangled Banner"?

Dennis

Kids Talk Jr.

COUNSELOR: Kendra

Dear Dennis,

People do these things out of respect for our country and for its history. Many people gave up their lives to give us the freedoms we have today. Every time you stand up for the pledge or the national anthem, you are showing respect.

Kendra

Kids Talk Jr.

COUNSELOR: Kendra

That's all the time I have for today. I have to get to dance class. I hope I answered all of your questions about respect. Turn the page to learn more about respect.

Sincerely,

Kendra

Grab a piece of paper and a pencil, and take this fun quiz. Good luck!

1. One way to respect the environment is to

    a) send it a card.

    b) pick up your trash.

    c) throw garbage on the ground.

2. Part of good manners is

    a) saying "please" and "thank you."

    b) yelling.

    c) breaking a lamp.

3. If you need to practice piano while your sister is watching TV, she should

    a) turn off the TV and find something else do.

    b) turn up the TV.

    c) hide all of your piano books.

4. Animals deserve respect

    a) sometimes.

    b) never.

    c) always.

5. If you are on someone else's property, you should

    a) respect it.

    b) destroy it.

    c) buy it.

6. If you know the answer in class, you should

    a) scream really loud.

    b) jump up and down.

    c) raise your hand.

7. It is important to respect other people's

    a) puppies.

    b) traditions.

    c) shoes.

8. To respect your body, you should

    a) rip a hole in your shirt.

    b) brush your teeth.

    c) never take a bath.

9. "Respect your elders" means that you respect

    a) older people like your grandparents.

    b) trees.

    c) hamsters.

10. When you say the Pledge of Allegiance, you should

    a) dance.

    b) run in place.

    c) stand.

ANSWER KEY:

1. b
2. a
3. a
4. c
5. a
6. c
7. b
8. b
9. a
10. c

Gaylord Nelson

Gaylord Nelson was a governor and senator from Wisconsin. He worked hard to create a day to celebrate the importance of respecting our environment. This day is called Earth Day.

On April 22, 1970, people all over the world took part in celebrating Earth Day. Teachers spent the day talking about respecting the environment. People planted trees and cleaned up litter from rivers and parks.

Earth Day is still celebrated all around the world. Thanks to Gaylord, people take the time to recycle, pick up trash, and celebrate our Earth.

Glossary

advice—opinions about what should or should not be done about a problem

disturb—to bother or annoy

elders—older people

environment—all of the trees, plants, water, and dirt

manners—polite and acting good

traditions—something a family has always done

To Learn More

AT THE LIBRARY

Kyle, Kathryn. *Respect.* Chanhassen, Minn.: Child's World, 2003.

Meiners, Cheri J. *Respect and Take Care of Things.* Minneapolis: Free Spirit Pub., 2004.

Raatma, Lucia. *Respect.* Mankato, Minn.: Bridgestone Books, 2000.

ON THE WEB

FactHound offers a safe, fun way to find Internet sites related to this book.

All of the sites on FactHound have been researched by our staff.

1. Visit *www.facthound.com*

2. Type in this special code
   for age-appropriate sites: 1404823182

3. Click on the FETCH IT button.

Your trusty FactHound will fetch the best sites for you!

Index

Look for all of the books in the Kids Talk Jr. series:

Kids Talk About Bravery	1-4048-2314-X
Kids Talk About Bullying	1-4048-2315-8
Kids Talk About Fairness	1-4048-2316-6
Kids Talk About Honesty	1-4048-2317-4
Kids Talk About Respect	1-4048-2318-2
Kids Talk About Sharing	1-4048-2319-0

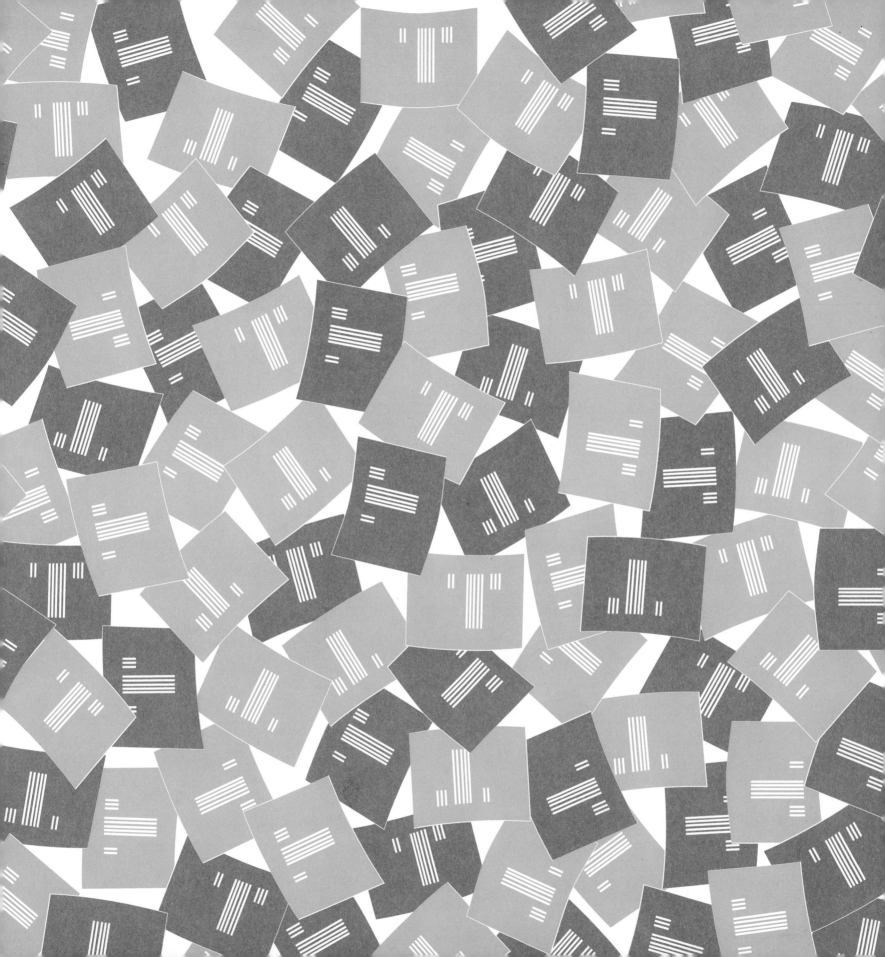